Secrets to Beat
MRI Claustrophobia

JESSIE LOPEZ

AuthorHouse™
1663 Liberty Drive
Bloomington, IN 47403
www.authorhouse.com
Phone: 1 (800) 839-8640

Because of the dynamic nature of the Internet, any web addresses or links contained in this book may have changed since publication and may no longer be valid. The views expressed in this work are solely those of the author and do not necessarily reflect the views of the publisher, and the publisher hereby disclaims any responsibility for them.

Any people depicted in stock imagery provided by Getty Images are models, and such images are being used for illustrative purposes only.
Certain stock imagery © Getty Images.

This book is printed on acid-free paper.

ISBN: 978-1-7283-6376-9 (sc)
ISBN: 978-1-7283-6377-6 (e)

Print information available on the last page.

Published by AuthorHouse

authorHOUSE®

To begin with, the first time you are faced with needing an MRI, don't panic. I'm sure many people have over-exaggerated what it's like to be in an MRI scanner. It is nothing more than just laying next to a big camera sitting above you. Nothing moves around you. It either sounds like a jack hammer or low-end dryer running.

The first time your doctor suggests you need a scan, be sure to let him know you are fearful. He will either prescribe you a sedative to take before your scan or you can be given one at the imaging center or department you go to. Try asking for an open MRI. Open scanners are much more comfortable for people with claustrophobia. They have the benefit of helping you overcome your fear.

The first thing you want to do is research on MRI. Find out as much as you can to understand that it's not all like people make it out to be. You will want to go by the facility or department where your scan will be and ask if you can see the scanner yourself. Imaging departments will let you see the machine because they want your business and will do whatever it takes to earn it. Your visualizations will help with your controlling fear, and we technicians can better steer it when you give us your trust. Try to make a list of questions before you go see the scanner. The more bases you cover, the better you will feel, making it easy to enter the scanner. Be sure the department or facility is aware of all your medical history and prescriptions you are taking. Also, MRI departments and facilities cannot supervise children so try to have a caretaker with you.

After scheduling your appointment, you will want to select some comfortable clothing. MRI exams require metal-free clothing. Wear sweatpants and a metal-free shirt. For women, a sports bra that has no metal is preferable. One reason for wearing loose clothing is it helps the technologist assist with your comfort level. No jewelry is allowed in the MRI room. Also, no pacemakers or electronic devices are allowed. The scanner is one big magnet, the kind that picks up cars in a wrecking yard. The soft tissue of your anatomy is safe next to a big magnet like this one, as long as there is no ferrous metal involved. Ferrous metal will be attracted to the magnet. So please try not to wear metal on your clothes. The technologist will dress you in a gown before your MRI exam. If you've had surgery and some metal placed in you, it's best to wait at least two months before a scan. It gives the metal time to grow into the body and keeps it from being attracted to the magnet, making it safer to scan. MRI compatibility cards are available from your surgeon and help with processing you safely.

Okay, so here we are. You are scheduled and have some knowledge of what to wear and if you'll be taking a sedative or not. You might want to bring a CD of your liking. Some MRI scanning rooms are compatible with music. We offer radio as well. You can find out that information when you view the scanning room prior to getting your exam scheduled. Remember, you are in control, so mindset is everything. Upon arrival, you will fill out paperwork about your medical history. If you are taking a sedative, you will need to have brought a driver.

The effects of the sedation will last for a few hours after the exam. Prior to taking a sedative, you probably should fast for four to six hours. The scheduling department should let you know this prior to you exam. The sedative relaxes your muscles and gives you the "I don't care" feeling. Be sure to arrive at least an hour early so the sedative will reach its full effect when it's time to scan. I jokingly like to tell my patients that it's the feeling of happy hour. You have the ability to relax and let your conscience go when under sedation. Some departments give sedation in IV form. That depends on your tolerance and severity of claustrophobia. Before your exam, a nurse or medic or even the technologist will set up an IV, preferably in your arm.

Now that you have filled out your paperwork and have been sedated, you will be asked by an MRI technologist to position yourself on a scanning table. As a reminder, most facilities do not supervise children unless they are getting a scan, so try to bring a caretaker. When being called for your exam by a technologist, be sure to make eye contact and shake the tech's hand. It is a proven fact that handshakes build trust between two parties. You'll want to start the trust with that first handshake. We technologists can feel your anxiety with a simple handshake. If you cannot shake our hand for personal reasons, we can sense it in your smile. Your claustrophobia is illuminated through that first impression, and we can see clearly that there needs to be special attention.

The MRI technologist will have you dress in a gown. Remember, metal-free clothing is what we are looking for. If you are having an exam that will include contrast, there will be an IV setup before the exam and contrast will be given before or during the scan. The IV will help the tech with the contrast injection; also it helps with added sedation or pain medication that you might need. For some patients, there may be blood drawn to check creatinine levels. Contrast is not suitable for people with kidney problems, so creatinine levels are checked to see if they are too high or too low. Be sure to let us know before your study of any complications you might be having in this area. After checking your blood—if needed—you will then lay down in a position suitable for the exam. I will show you photographs of patient positions later in this book. You can work on your mindset once you see how little confinement there is. Be sure you tell the tech before your scan that you want communication during each sequence of the exam. I'll explain sequences later on.

Now that you have been educated a little and prepped for your scan, here is where I let you in on the MRI technologist's secrets to beating claustrophobia. First, our golden rule is to stay still during your exam. There will be a couple of moments where we will let you stretch an arm or leg, but not many. Your position is vital when slicing in millimeters on a computer. If you move while we are scanning your anatomy, there will be minutes added to you exam. Movement produces shadowing images on our screen, and a radiologist finds that unacceptable when reading your scan.

I mentioned sequences earlier. Sequences are the times you hear the scanner making noise between every quiet moment. Each sequence lasts between three to seven minutes. Your exam can last thirty minutes to an hour depending on your doctor's orders. Once you have told the MRI tech that you want communication between sequences, we know for sure you are highly claustrophobic and need that extra attention during your scan. Between sequences, we will communicate so that you know there is always someone watching you. We will offer you a towel to cover your eyes if possible. We will then begin to play music of your liking. One key is to set the mood of a relaxed atmosphere. Open MRI scanners can set this mood perfectly. Closed scanners can provide this as well. Most departments will have a window to look out of. It is up to the individual and how much you let us work with you. Remember, you are in control. Be sure you tell the tech you want total communication. I cannot express this enough.

Once we have started to scan and have completed the first sequence, we will ask you, "How are you doing? How is your comfort level?" There will be talk between us, and then we will tell you we are proceeding with the next sequence, which will last another three to seven minutes. We will do this throughout the whole exam. We will always communicate between sequences and can tell you how much longer the next one will last. That is the key. You will always know what is going on and know there is a communication line open at all times.

For contrast studies, after about thirty minutes we may pull you out to inject the contrast. You will still be in your position, but you cannot get up or move much because the scanner already has your anatomical position set in its memory. So don't move when we pull you out. Try to stay still until we give you the okay to move a leg or arm for comfort. Once your injection is done, we will send you back into the scanner in the same position you were in to begin with. We will scan you for another ten to fifteen minutes with the contrast highlighting the pathology. During this post-contrast study, we will again talk to you during the sequences of the scan. Once we are finished, we will pull you out and take your vitals if needed. A nurse or medic will give you instructions for the rest of the day.

To beat this claustrophobia, there has to be total communication before, during, and after each sequence. The secret is that between those sequences, someone is always talking to you.

Remember, claustrophobia is a fear of no one being there to help you, and we techs cover that base well. We are here to help, always watching, and are very experienced in dealing with MRI claustrophobia.

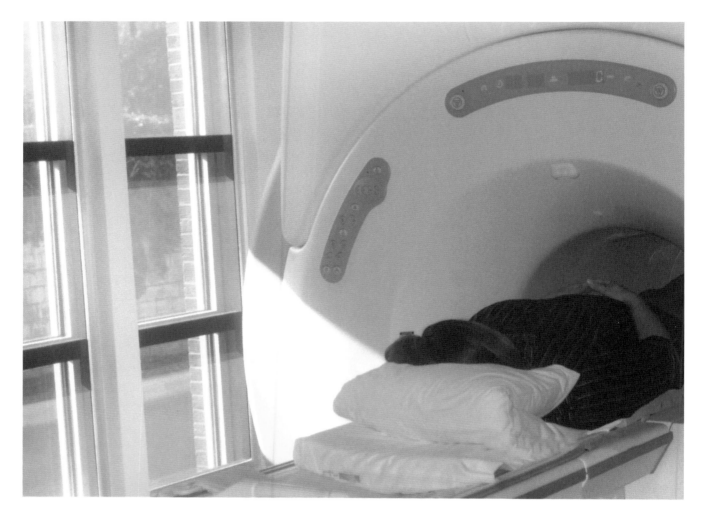

High Field (Closed Scanner)
Patient Position: Knee, lower leg, ankle, foot, pelvis, abdomen

This position shows how the patient is halfway out of the scanner. She is listening to music and looking outside. Some departments have a window next to the scanner. The tech is behind her, on the other side of a window, using a microphone for communication. The patient will also be given a call bell to hold on to in case she wants to alert the tech that she wants to come out immediately.

Reminder: she might be sedated.

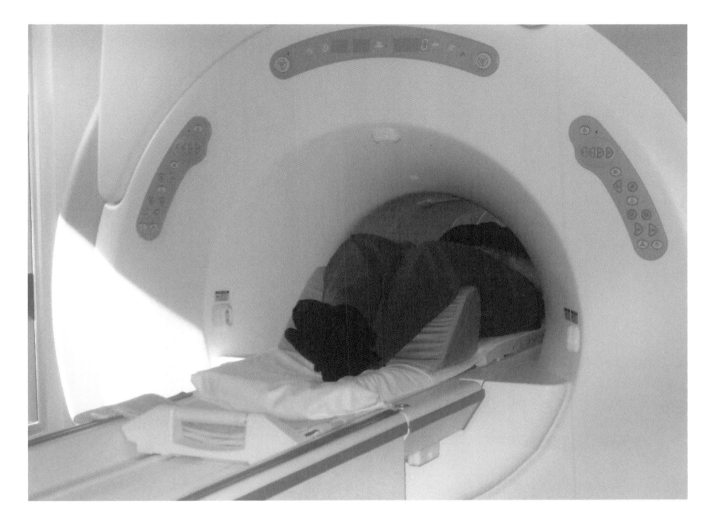

High Field (Closed Scanner)
Patient Position: Brain, eyes, neck, thoracic spine, shoulder, lumbar spine, abdomen, pelvis

When doing a hand or wrist exam, you will most likely be on your stomach in a Superman position, going in headfirst. In some departments, the patient in this position will have headphones to listen to music. The patient still has communication through a microphone imbedded in the scanner and a call bell to alert the tech of sudden onset of claustrophobia. When doing a brain scan, the patient will have a coil around her head. It looks somewhat like a helmet. When doing a cervical scan (neck), the patient will have a coil over her face that grabs images of the neck. The patient can always have a washcloth over her eyes, and sedation is ultimately an option. You will see the helmet and cervical coil in my open scanner photos later in this book.

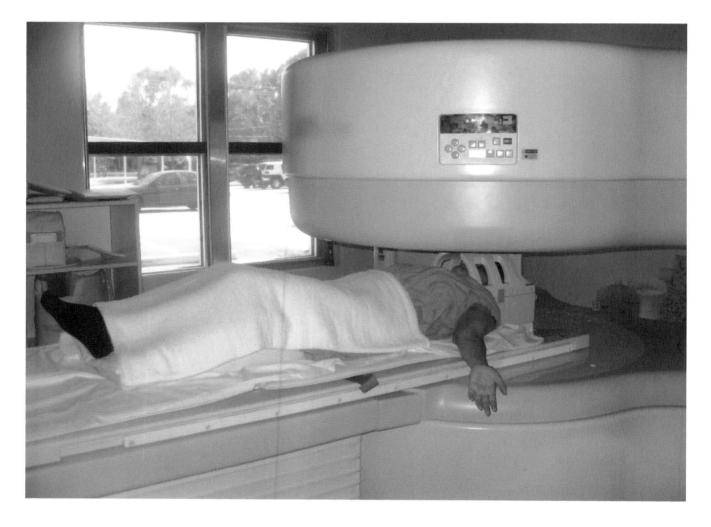

Open MRI (Low Field)
Patient Position: Brain scan, IAC, pituitary, orbit, etc.

Notice the spacing between the body and the scanner. The patient's arms are out to show the open area surrounding patient. There is no sense of confinement. The patient is listening to music and feeling very relaxed in an open area. She might even be sedated. The tech is behind a window, in total communication with the patient through a microphone embedded in the scanner. This brain scan shows the type of helmet that is most likely used in a high-field scanner. Remember, the patient can have a washcloth over her eyes as well. When it comes to injecting contrast, the tech will go in and inject it, preferably in the arm that has the most palpable veins, and then resume the post scan.

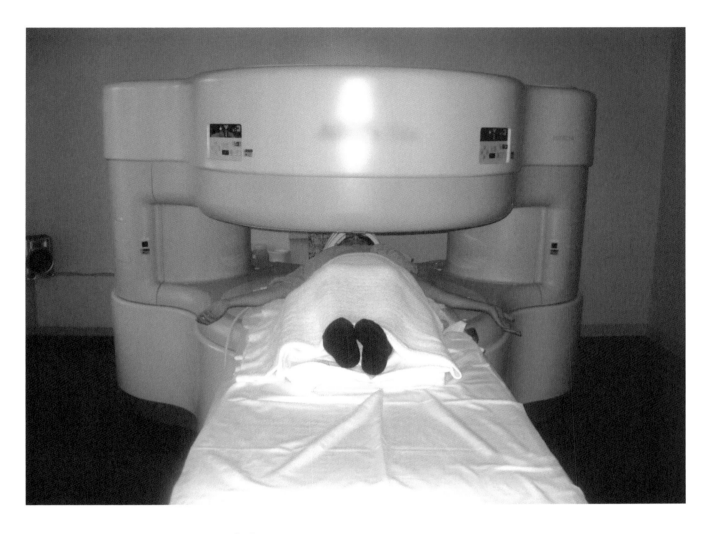

Open MRI (Low Field)
Patient Position: Brain scan, IAC, pituitary, orbit, etc.

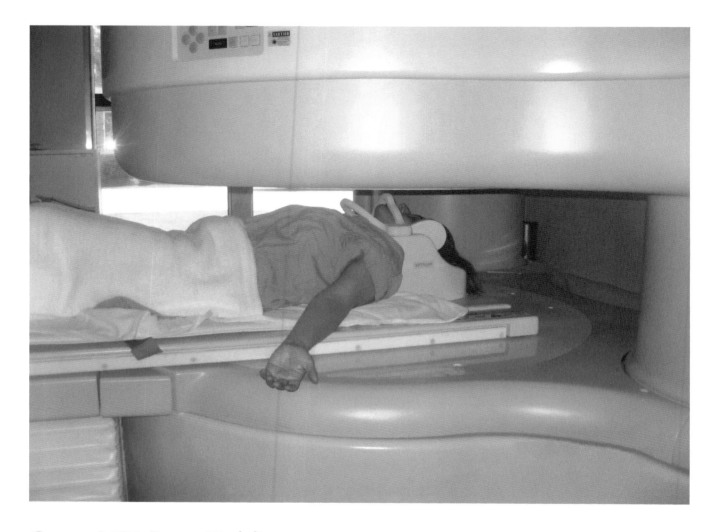

Open MRI (Low Field)
Patient Position: Cervical (neck), soft tissue, carotids, etc.

Notice how the patient's face is not totally covered up. The patient's arms are out to show the open area surrounding the patient. There is no sense of confinement. The patient is listening to music and feeling very relaxed in an open area. She even might be sedated and can always have a washcloth over her eyes if she wishes. The tech is behind a window in total communication with the patient through a microphone embedded in the scanner. This coil over the neck looks like what is used for high-field cervical scans.

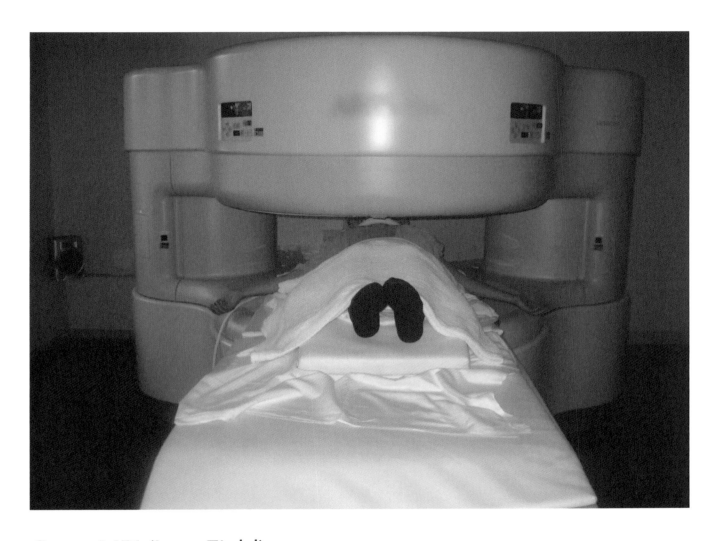

Open MRI (Low Field)
Patient Position: Cervical (neck), soft tissue, carotids, etc.

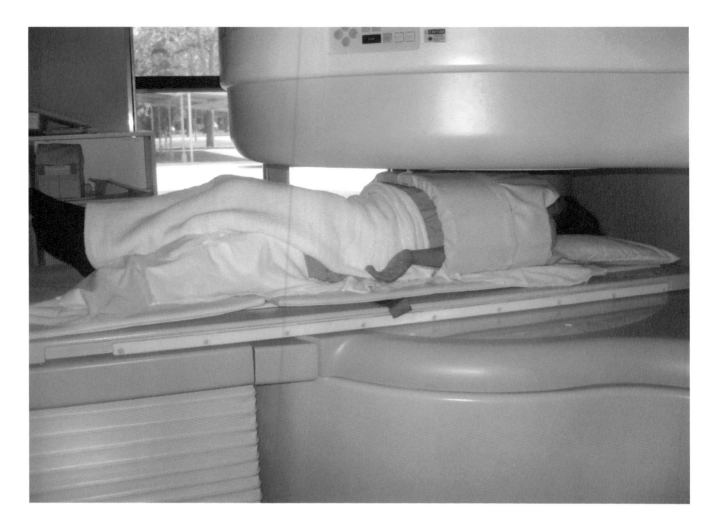

Open MRI (Low Field)
Patient Position: Thoracic spine, clavicle, chest, etc.

Notice the space surrounding the patient. She is also listening to music and aware of the tech speaking to her at the same time. She can turn her head and look out the window for extra comfort. Her eyes can be covered, and don't forget that she can have sedation if needed. This position can also let the patient have her arms above her head and give the patient a sense of not having her body entirely covered.

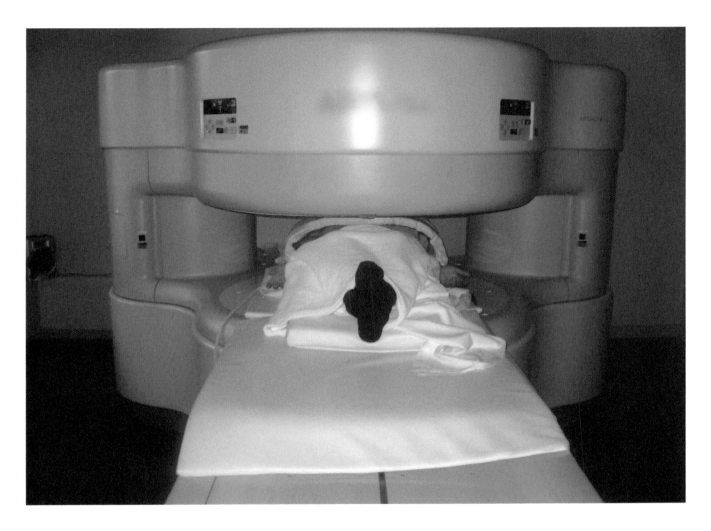

Open MRI (Low Field)

Patient Position: Thoracic spine, clavicle, chest, etc.

The patient has all the benefits of an open area.

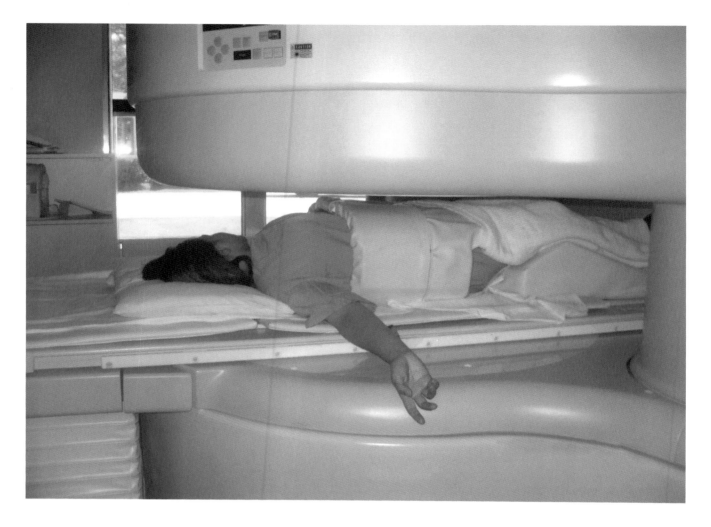

Open MRI (Low Field)
Patient Position: Lumbar spine, abdomen, pelvis, hips, etc.

The lumbar, abdomen, pelvis, and hips can either go in head first or feet first. I preferably like to send the patient in feet first. It gives her the comfort of not seeing her face covered up first when going in. Notice the space surrounding the patient. She is also listening to music and aware of the tech speaking to her at the same time. She can turn her head and look out the window for extra comfort. Don't forget there can be sedation and an eye covering if needed. The patient also has support under her legs for added comfort to the spine.

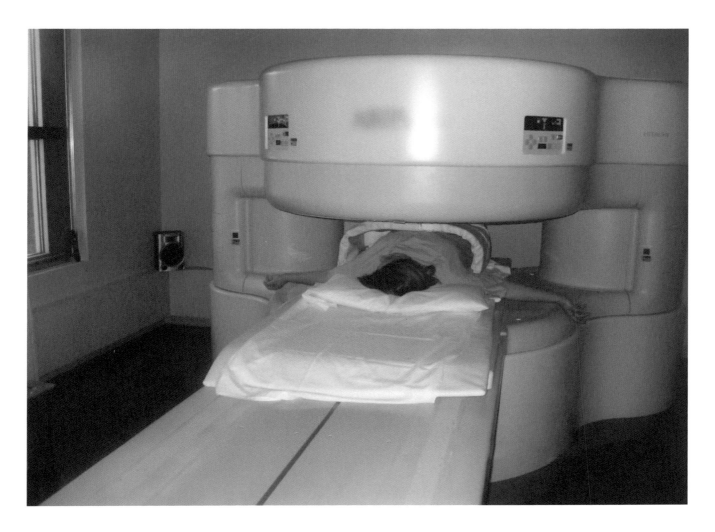

Open MRI (Low Field)

Patient Position: Lumbar spine, abdomen, pelvis, hips, etc.

Notice the open area all around the patient.

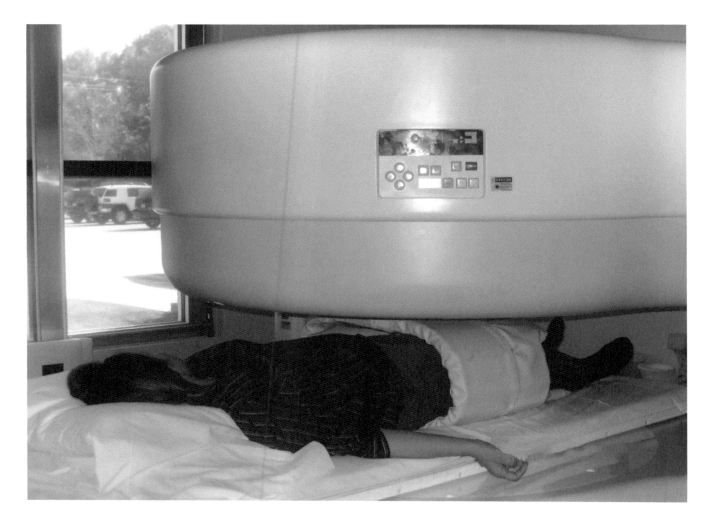

Open MRI (Low Field)
Patient Position: Upper legs (femur), knees

All benefits remain the same as the above-mentioned situations. This coil is a body coil and can be used for the lower leg and larger knees if needed. Notice how the head is out from under the scanner. Positions like this sometimes call for taping the feet together. A patient will move unconsciously, without thinking. It's common nature to move when laying on your back too long. Communication is always there, even if a patient is halfway out.

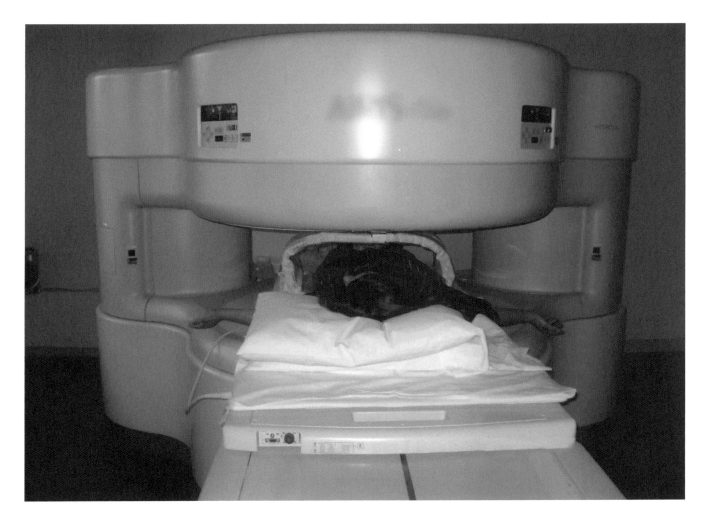

Open MRI (Low Field)
Patient position: Upper legs (tibia/fibula), knees

Notice all the area between the patient and the coil. For some patients, this area is essential due to the size of the patient. For bigger patients, the coil would fit like a belt.

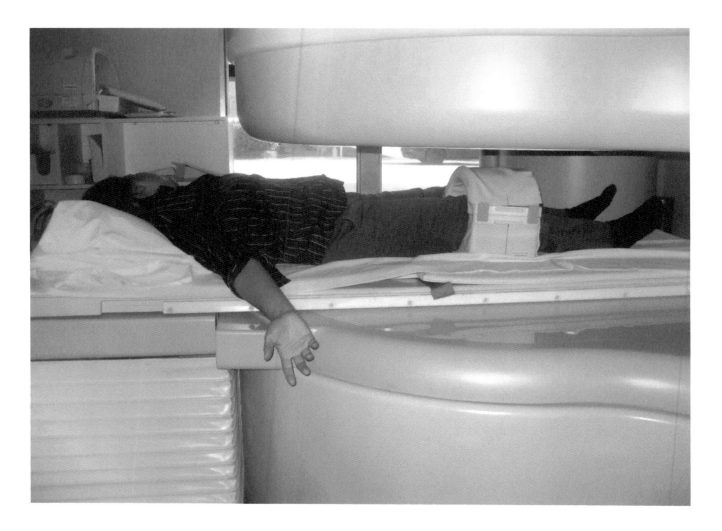

Open MRI (Low Field)
Patient Position: Right or left knee

All benefits remain the same. Also notice the patient is halfway out due to the knee coil being in the middle of the scanner for highest signal. Always remember that even in this position, a patient can have sedation, an eye covering, or whatever it takes to comfort the patient.

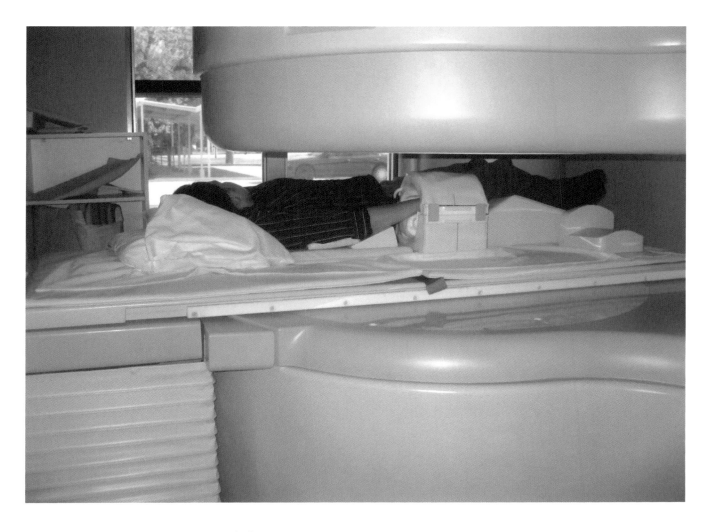

Open MRI (Low Field)
Patient Position: Hand, wrist, or sometimes arm

All the benefits are the same. The patient is a little farther in but has the same feeling of not being confined. Notice the cushion under the legs for added comfort to the spine. Remember, for heavy claustrophobia, the patient can have a washcloth. We technologist will do whatever we can to make the patient comfortable, and communication is always there.

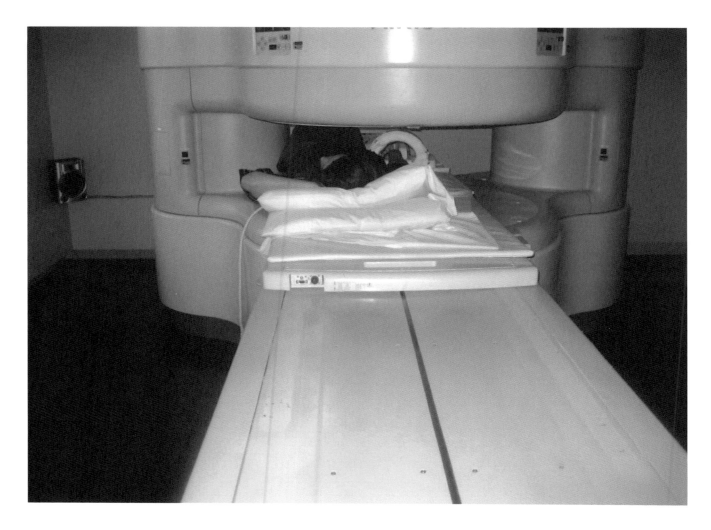

Open MRI (Low Field)
Patient Position: Hand, wrist, or sometimes arm

I cannot stress enough the open area that an open scanner can give the patient. The benefits remain the same as stated before.

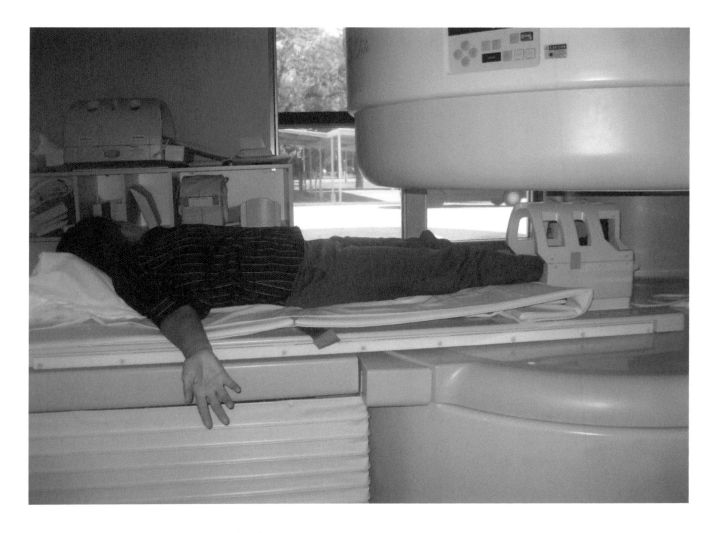

Open MRI (Low Field)
Patient Position: Ankle, foot, etc.

There are different coils we use for these positions. In this position, I used a head coil. I like the signal I get with this coil. All techs use different coils according to their own preference. Notice how the patient is more than halfway out of the scanner. All benefits remain the same. There is no confinement. The patient can also have some cushioning under her knees for comfort to the spine, but not much.

Thank you for buying my e-book. This is the first book that I've ever written. I have so much information I want to share to help people. I will be looking into seminars or counseling to share this information in the future. I am definitely going to publish a paperback book of this information, so it will be the first of many more to come. I will stay in touch with those who buy this book to give them more in-depth information on claustrophobia. I'm looking into business online, so I guarantee you that what I put out on the net or on paper will definitely benefit you in every way imaginable.

Thanks again for your time, and God bless you and your family.

Jessie Lopez
Certified MRI Technologist

About the Author

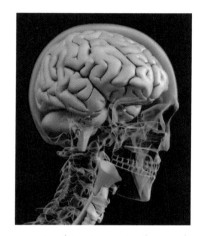

Hello, my name is Jessie E. Lopez. I wrote an e-book giving away the secrets we technologist use to beat claustrophobia in a closed and open MRI scanners. I first want to tell you about myself so you know I have extensive knowledge about MRI claustrophobia. I have been in the imaging field for about six years now; during my first three years, I worked as a radiographer. I learned many techniques for keeping patients calm and relaxed during an MRI exam. As a radiographer, one year I also did work as an MRI tech assistant. I prepped, sedated, and positioned patients, and injected contrast for the technologist. I began to learn how to talk a patient into beating his claustrophobia. I was then asked by another facility if I wanted to train to learn how to scan, free of charge. I saw it as an opportunity to start a career in the closed and open MRI field. I had trained on two scanners, where I consistently talked people out of their fears. I then studied physics to become an MRI technologist. I became certified and have over ten thousand hours in my current career. At the moment, I feel I have mastered the art of beating claustrophobia in closed and open MRI scanners. I want to share my experience with you and anybody who wishes to take a moment to read my e-book to better equip themselves for their exam. I'm spilling the beans on our secrets of how we get a fearful patient through a scan.

In my e-book, I will reveal secrets we technologists use to get claustrophobic patients through their scan. I will go in depth on how a patient can overcome his fear after having an MRI done. I will explain patient positioning for each part of the body and whether the face will be exposed or not. I will show photographs of each position we do for every part of the body and how the feeling of confinement will vanish with a few simple techniques. I will show open and closed units and let you see how some positions are really not all that confined. I've found open scanners to be way more useful for MRI claustrophobia. Almost all my patients get through their exam with the helpful techniques I share before and during their exams.

Thank you for ordering my very first E-book. I'm going to pour my heart out on this one and hopefully start to write many more on other subjects. So take some time out, sit down, get comfortable, and be ready for some need-to-know information by an honest, hardworking MRI technologist who cares about claustrophobic patients.

NOTES BEFORE EXAM